Songs from the Heart

Songs from the Heart

A Window to My Silent Thoughts

Catrina De jong Parkinson

Library of Congress Control Number:		2011903537
ISBN:	Hardcover	978-1-4568-8192-4
	Softcover	978-1-4568-8191-7
	Ebook	978-1-4568-8193-1

To order additional copies of this book, contact:
Xlibris Corporation
0-800-644-6988
www.xlibrispublishing.co.uk
Orders@xlibrispublishing.co.uk
301771

Contents

Dad and Mum
Uncle Dennis
Camilla
My Husband and Children
You are my rock and Inspiration
I could not have done it without you

My children

When God made you
He knew what he was doing
He took a bit of Daddy
And he took a bit of me
He mixed it all together
And then he thought what next!
He gave you some character
And your very own mined
He filled you up with love
And a wonderful great big smile

When he sent you of to me
I just couldn't believe my luck
Such an amazing and wonderful gift
The Lord had given me
His most beautiful creations
Especially for me
I treasure each one of you
And keep you close to my heart
Never forgetting you came to me, from up above
Love mum

When you were a baby

When you were a baby
You stayed close by my side
Always looking to me for assurance
If mum gave a smile
You knew it was safe
Mum was your hero
She knew all that their ever was to know
She had all the answers that you could ever need
When you were hungry, she pulled out a snack
When you were thirsty she held out some juice
When you were tired she rocked you to sleep
When you fell down she gave you a cuddle and kiss
Mum had all the answers that you could ever need
But when you're all grown, and need me know more
You go where you want, and do as you please
You are your own boss, with lots of things you can do
I'll still be there
Whenever and were ever you need me
Love mum

Tears of Joy

I opened my eyes
And there you were
The nurse holding you up to my face
I stared at you in love and awe
Such pure perfection
Yet you seemed so vulnerable
So scared of this your new life
But you have me!
I took you up into my arms
And held you close up to my heart
I felt your little body
So warm so soft
My eyes misted up
I felt happiness so deep
So inexplicable yet real
My face was wet
As the tears fell down from my eyes
Tears of joy
Tears of utmost happiness

You are my children

My children do you not know
Do you not see that your pain is mine too?
I am your mother; I carried you for nine months
I woke up night after night to feed you
I changed you diapers and nappies
I cried when you got your first injection
When you got sick I worried like crazy
And all through that I loved you more and more
To me you are all my children
And I love each and every one
Do you know how much it hurts me?
When you think I favor one over another
That is never my intention
I feel for each and every one of you
And I know each one of you is special
And therefore your needs are different
I know your strengths and weaknesses
And I know who needs me more at times
You are not the same in your needs
Neither are you the same in your souls
Each of you came at a different time
And each of you has a different path
So you must appreciate your difference
Rather than compare your selves
It is these differences that make you all special
Please know that I love you all
You mean so much to me
More than you could ever know

To My Dearest Son

When I think of you I feel so proud
So proud of whom you are
And what you have achieved
You are such a special soul
You have such amazing determination
Filled with love and ambition
I see a side that most may not
A softer, gentler side to you
The one that gives you your perfect balance
To help you make some of life's decisions
In times and days that come your way
You bring with you so many gifts
That comes to us in many forms
From the way you tease and how you joke
To the way you think and how you talk
Bringing to me such pride and joy
To see how far, you've come your way
Remember now and every day
I love you more than words can ever say

She's your baby girl

When you hold that baby in your arms
Look in to her eyes
Can you see how much she needs you?
Do you see how much she trusts you?
Her little life is in your hands
So precious and so fragile
Show her you love her
That you will always be there
Make sure you guide her
Through her stages of growth
She needs your compassion
And lots of devotion
She's your little baby
But time goes so fast
Soon she'll be a lady out to a dance
And if you brought her up well
You'll have nothing to worry
But if you did not
Then that's another story

To a special girl

You are such a special girl
The best daughter I could ever have
And I knew this from the day that you were born
You had the cutest face and smile
And the older you grew the more I new
Just what a special soul that you are
You bring with you a gentleness and love
You have such a mature understanding
One you need to nurture and keep growing
As this will help guide you some day
You care so much for those around you
And this makes you such a dear
It's what connects all those around you
By a string invisible to the eye
Only seen by those that care
Those who know you are so dear
My special dear, little girl
I love the way you show you care
In the little things you do for me
It means so much to know your there
Bringing me such warm affection
Remember now and every day
I love you more than words can ever say

To my little boy

You are so amazing to me
So much so that I cannot help loving you so
You are and have always been
My dear little boy
When I think of you I have to smile
You are so full of curiosity
A curiosity that never leaves you
And grows with you day by day
In you I see a gentle soul
A soul with love and much compassion
This I see in how you act and what you say
But strength you have, I know and see
In what you say and what you do
You can hold your own and stand your ground
When an if you feel the need
I love the little gifts you bring
The flowers and twigs you pick for me
They let me know you love me so
Remember now and every day
That I love you more than words can ever say

Who can be mum

Anyone can be a mother
But how many can be a mum?
Being a mum means being there
Through the whole journey
The joys and sorrows
The troubles and confusions
Being a mum means stepping up to the plate
It means you show that they matter
Not only by what you say but that, that you do
It's the choices you make
The decisions you take
Children know more than you think
So rise to the challenge
And show you are mum
You may need to say "No"
But that's coz you dare
If it's done out of love
They know that you care

Mum's my name

Mum, is my name
Mum is the word I hear calling to me
I hear it in the morning and in the afternoon
I hear it at night and even my dreams
Mum is the word that fills my house
I hear it in the bathroom and in the bedroom
I hear it from the kitchen and even the lounge
"Mum" yes, that's me
I am a cook, a teacher
A doctor, therapist
Toy mechanic, scientist
Artist, consultant
And even a friend
I need to have answers to all of these fields
Even if I have never trained in any of them
My days are long and my pay comes in many forms
Some times in hugs
But also in cards
In kisses and flowers
Smiles and pasta rings
But most of all
The love in those twinkling eyes

A Mother's Love

A mother's love is like a circle
It has no beginning, no ending
It asks for little but gives much
A mother's love is universal
It knows no language, no country
A mother's love has no fear
It will fight, it will conquer
To protect the precious child
A mother's love is so strong
It moves mountains and bridges
A mother's love can be felt
She is the warmth, the softness
That fills up your soul

A Love So Fresh and Pure

You are so special to me
More than you could ever know
The sound of your voice
Brings so much joy to my heart
The sound of your little foot steps
Fills me with a warm and fuzzy feeling inside
Your soft chubby cheeks close to my face
And sticky hands holding me tight
Such pure love that you give to me
Who could ask for anything more
I hold you close in my arms
I sing you a song
A song from my heart
One filled with loves sweet melodies
You are so gentle and cuddly to hold
You bring to me, the world's greatest joy
And a love that only you could ever give
A love of a mother and child
So fresh, so warm, so pure

Mothers of the world

Mothers of the world, we salute you
You are such an amazing being
You have so much strength
You have so much will
So much love
You sacrifice all for your family
Day in and day out
You go by your day with little complaints
You never think twice
You hold every one up
Giving all that you have
Oh mother of the world you are, our hero
You carry our children
You give birth to life
You nurture all of us
Where do you get your strength?
What drives you each day?
You are the back bone of society
Yet few people acknowledge you
Or give you any credit
Oh mothers of the world you are our lives
Without you were would we be?
Who would take care of us?
Who would make us feel special?
Who would teach us faith?
Who would give us hope?
Who would give us a soul?

Daddy and Mummy

You gave me life
You gave me love
You gave me hope
You gave me passion
I came in to the world, but a scared little girl
And you were there to hold my hand
I came in this world with a desire to be loved
And you took care of me and gave me love
I came in to this world with dreams of my own
And you gave me the freedom to keep my hope alive
I came in to this world with a passion for art
And you allowed me to keep my flame burning
It is because of this that I too;
Can give life
Can give love
Can give hope
And give passion
Thank you
Catrina

The child within

Can you see the little child in all of us?
Yes the little child we try to hide
At times we do it well and no one knows she's there
But every once in a while the little child comes out
Whenever we lose control then we let her out
We shout, we cry, we throw tantrums
We feel so out of control just like we did as a child
We feel scared, of how this makes us feel
It feels like we did when we were small
When we had such little control
Don't feel scared, to show your feelings
Let her out; let her cry her heart out
Just open out your arms to her and let her know you care
Let her feel that it's ok to feel that way
She needs to know you understand, just how it makes her feel
She needs to feel you care for her, and then she'll go away
She needs to feel the love you have, so she can stay inside
For when there is love inside, then she feels your there
Then there is no need to shout, no need to feel so scared
So find the love inside and all is calm and within

My soul mate

Do you ever wonder how it all happened?
How did we end up together?
Could it be luck or could it be fate
Was it our destiny to be together?
You made me feel special
You made me feel cute
I knew that I'd love you forever
It felt like we were always meant to be
Like two seeds in a pod
We fitted together so well
You were everything I wanted and more
You made me feel so secure
So free and so complete
I was in love, in love with you
In love with the way you made me feel
Never had I felt so safe
I knew then you were the one
The one who would marry me
You would be the father of my children
The one I would live with for rest of my life
Yes, I knew this deep in my heart and deep in my soul
We were made for each other
And like a magnet we had attracted the other
Our energy just fusing as one
Beating to the same rhythm
The same beat
Some people cast doubt
But we knew better, we knew the truth
And here we are decades later
Still together and still so sure
We were made for the other
And not any other

Techno baby

Is it not scary?
How fast that things change?
Dose it not bother you
Where life will be tomorrow?
No sooner do you have the latest gadget
Than it changes once more
No sooner do you learn how to use it
Than a new one comes to light
Can we really keep moving at such a rate?
Surely something will topple it down
For what goes up must come down
Is this not too much too soon?
Will not life become too much of a burden?
With so many new things to learn
Won't babies get depression?
Will people have no babies?
Will we buy them grown and educated?
Or programmed in to the latest phone
Is that were we're heading too?
Dose that not make you wary
To me that sounds so scary
When will it ever end?
Where do we draw the line?

Soul sister

The thought of leaving you brings tears to my eyes
You have been such a good friend to me
You celebrated with me the joys of my life
And mourned the sorrows that came by
When in doubt it's you that I called
To give me the courage that carried me through
You never betrayed me or gave up on me
Time after time I'd come to you
With all my burdens and my troubles
And there you were
Smile on your face and open arms
You know that meant so much to me
It took any sadness or pain away
It gave me so much needed love and care
It made me feel that I mattered too
It gave so much needed confidence
It gave me a feeling of warmth in my heart
You are so much more than a friend to me
You are my soul sister

The friends I have

The friends I have are few
But the ones I have are true
They are there for me in times of joy
And in times of need and sorrow
They are with me when I want
And even when I don't
I know they always mean the best
By how they put my heart to rest
It's what they say and what they do
They show me who they really are
No masks and no pretence
I cherish these friends I have
I need not ask for more

The joys of my heart

I sit and I smile, a thought, an image
I need to create what's in my mind
A paper and pencil, that's all I need,
Time goes by as I put thought to paper
I hear nothing and see nothing
My mind drifts to another place, another time
My mind fills with peace, with passion
I continue to create from my heart
My pencil moves across the paper
This way and that way as though on its own
Slowly by slowly an image appears
First is the eyes and then all the rest
I sit back and I smile at the picture before me
Where was it, how did it come
It was always there I just let it out
I allowed it to come out by using my pencil
I am but a tool that gives life to a picture
I use my eyes and my heart to let it all out
It gives me such joy, such absolute pleasure
To do what I do
I thank the oh Lord for this gift that I have
I thank the oh Lord for the joy that it brings
To see people smile at something I drew
To share my love, to share my passion
Is truly a blessing, a gift from above?

The voiceless people

Do you see them standing there?
Those are people, people without a voice
They are our silent brothers, our silent sisters
The shadows of society
They walk by and nobody sees them
They go hungry and nobody cares
When they are sick nobody treats them
The faceless people
We see these people every day
The assistant, the mother, the cleaner
They have feelings just like you
The people without a voice
Stop, take time and acknowledge them
It doesn't hurt to greet and smile
Open your eyes see them
Listen to their story
Who knows it might be just like yours
These are people just like you
They have families and children too
They are living souls
It takes one kind act to change a life
But the inspiration can turn a city
And later turn the world

What you do to me

I smile because of my love for you
My world has more meaning than ever before
Because of you I feel whole once more
I cherish every moment with you
I can't wait to see you each day
Just so that I can be with you
I bask in the rays of your every praise
I am a better person because of you
You bring out my true emotions
Because of you I can smile again
I can live through troubled times
Knowing you will be there with me
You bring light to my soul
You light up my world

Is it a dream?

I have a dream for tomorrow
A dream of my life, as it should be
I see a great big mansion that's so lovely to see
It has so many windows and so may rooms
I can see a long drive way with so many flowers
There's a butler and maid waiting on me
Oh my, what a great big entrance and amazing staircase
I walk to the top and down the long corridor
Is that my room my such Wondrous beauty
I walk to the window and take a look out
The yard is so huge and such lovely big trees
I love the little stream and the ducks in the pond
Look at the gardens is that all for me
I see down to the little cottages were my staff live
Such a beautiful path with pebbles and grass
Then I hear "Mam?" I realize that's me
It's no longer a dream, it is my life now
Oh how amazing that my dream has come true
But how could it not, as I knew that it would
If you believe it, it's yours, that's what I learnt
So here I go to enjoy my new life
With my beloved family right by my side
Oh what a wonderful day that it is

Aren't We All Lucky?

My mind is full of things, things I should do
It feels so confusing up inside of my head
Time is running out and I don't know what to do
It seems like there's no way to get it all done
I know what I want, but not how to do it
Should I do this or should I do that?
Should I go hear or should I go there?
These are the questions going round in my head
Every day gone, is another day lost
One day less to get things done
I try to be positive and let it all go
It's up to the universe, to get it for me
The universe knows just what I need
It feels kind of silly to just let it all go
But what can I say it seems to be working
Maybe I'll rest and let it just be

Give a Dream

What is a life without a dream?
To have no reason and no purpose
To go around with no spirit
To look and yet see nothing
How sad that must be
So to give a dream is to breathe life
To give reason and a purpose
To give passion and desire
To give site to the blind
Lucky are you who can give
Share what you can, with those with none
A small gift may mean more, to another
Even a smile or a simple nod
This gives meaning
This gives purpose

Listen to the heart

To listen with your heart is but a special gift
To hear the unspoken words of the heart
To feel the emotion in the eyes
To see beyond the spoken words
To sense beyond the mind
Is but a gift that comes from the heart
It's something that's hard to put in words
And something that's hard to explain
It's a feeling or a hunch
That feels so strong you know it's true
So true you feel compelled to act
And it's that act that makes it so special

Hope

What is life without hope?
Hope is what carries us by
It's what we look to when we are down
It gives us the will to go on
It helps us plan for tomorrow
Hope gives us courage to speak out
It helps us believe things can change
Without hope what would we have?
Hope helps to dry our tears
Hope gives us a second chance
And what's best is it costs nothing
It's free, free for all of us
All we need is a little time
To sit back and clear our minds
Then we are able to see that there's hope
Hope for tomorrow, hope for our sorrow
Just open your eyes and see what you have
See what matters deep in your heart
You have hope and now you have strength
So lift up your head and soldier on
You are much braver than you ever imagined
And now you too, can give hope to others
Because you have done it,
So will others

My life the illusion

Is life but a simple delusion?
Could it be but a kind of a dream?
Do I really own what I have?
Or is it just a life of fiction
Am I as mighty as I feel
Or is that also an illusion
What am I if not what I own?
Who am I if not my possessions?
Can life be real or am I too an illusion?
I feel that my thoughts and feeling are more real
More real than all that I see
More real than all that I own
My thoughts are mine
They stay with me no matter what
It is these thoughts that create
They bring about the illusion
They bring to me all that I think
So then, they are real!
What I have and what I own are illusions
Illusions of my thoughts
So with this I can be
With this I can have
And knowing this, gives me power
It gives me the power, to create and enjoy
To enjoy my life, my illusion

The cross roads of my life

I'm sited at the cross roads of my life
And I know just what, I should be doing
I need to make some big choices
Of where to go and what I must do
To bring out the hidden, diamond with in
To give me what I have longed in my life
The life I dreamt of day and night
My future and my destiny
It's all in the mined and all up to me
So here I go with passion and dreams
Some think I'm crazy and others just laugh
But I know I can and I know I will
Just give some time and you'll see how I fly
High in the sky like a bird up in flight
Ill sore like an eagle there's no stopping me
I believe in myself, and that's all I need

I have the power

There was a time when I lived in fear
Fear to speak out, against things I didn't like
Fear to share my thoughts and feelings
Fear to stand up, for my rights and those I loved
I never wanted to hurt any one
I felt like it was my duty to be tolerant
To keep the peace around me
To put others needs before my own
But then I grew up, I woke up one day
Yes, I realized the power was mine
I had a strength that I never knew existed
I felt the power moving within me
Giving me the strength
And it was this day that I stood up
It was this day that I spoke out for what I believe
I made it known, that never again, would I hide
Never again, would I look the other way
I would stand for those I love and cared for
I would fight for their rights, in every way
For as long as it would take
I have the power, I have the strength.

My Thoughts My World

The power of thought belongs to all
It's one of the most powerful things we posses
The driving force living in you
It starts with a flick of light a subtle idea
And before you know it your intension is out
You don't have to know it or how it will be
Like a magnet you start to attract it to you
Slowly it's coming together for you
While you are sleeping even washing your hair
From the smallest of mundane things that you do
To the chance meetings taking place
Your thoughts are creating the desire of your heart
Some people know this yet others do not
And that matters little as it works just the same
If you're lucky enough you can watch it all happen
Witnessing as it appears before your very eyes
A though in your mind and now you can feel it
A thought in your mind and now it's your world

Dream Big It's Free

If you dare to dream make sure it's big
Don't hold back just let it all out?
The cost need not matter as it's not for you to worry
It's up for your taking whatever it is
And it's got nothing to do with your life situation
You just have to feel it and know that it's there
Once your mined can believe that you know that it's yours
But don't you stop there do everything else
As you would if you had it right this very day
The more passion you have the faster it comes
The universe cares little whom that you are
All it needs is the song from your heart
With feelings, belief and all of your trust
It's your for the taking just accept that it's yours
Hold out your hands and claim what is your
Your dream is yours believe that for sure
The song from your heart
And yes you deserve it
Because you dared to dream

My Day of Freedom

I wake up and open my eyes
I look around and what do I see?
Oh no! Why oh why oh why?
When will it end?
When will I leave this place?
I lie in my bed and listen to the sounds
The sound of madness coming from the corridor
I hear loud yawns, doors opening and banging
Feet go shuffling up and down constantly
I need peace! I need to sleep!
But I can't, not while I'm here
Try as I may it's the same each day
I keep telling myself; it will all come to an end
My day to leave will be soon
But each day comes and goes
Still I wait for my day of freedom
I have to be strong
I have to hold on
My day is near
I feel it coming soon
The day I shall walk out of this place
Free of this madness
The madness I called home

Bitter sweet destiny

Is it really time to go?
Are those my tickets and luggage?
Is that plane really there for me?
It feels so surreal
I turn around and feel the tears
I try and try to hold back
But soon they just burst out
My emotions so mixed up
I 'm crying out of joy
But also out of pain
Such a bitter sweet day
I'm happy to take my children
Yet sad to leave my parents
So sad to say goodbye
I want the pain to go away
The guilt within my heart
I look towards my children
But still I fall apart
I'm feeling so confused
So full of mixed emotions
I try once more to hold it back
But then I just let go
I let it all come pouring out
It's what I need to do
I burst out crying with all I have
I cry and cry as I say good bye
Tears pouring down my face
It's all I can do right now
Just let it all out
It's a new life now pulling
And I'm right in its path
My children are calling
My journey begins!

My Data entry work

I wake up and start the same process all over again
I sit on my computer and begin my search
I'm looking for work, can that be so hard?
I go from search to search, looking from town to town
And if I do find some work I can do
I now have to enter my details
Page after page I enter my details
But that's not the end
Every time I click on to Next
Up pops a pop up in red
Saying I haven't completed
So back I go and try and correct it
I do this not once, but over and over again
After hours and hour's sore figures and back
I finally come to the end
But lo and behold the page won't go through
I started at morning and now its noon
How can computers determine my fate?
How many times do I have to this a day
Why can't I just write on a paper and post it to them?
What if I don't own a computer?
I've been at this for months
And still not a chance of a position for me
Nobody told me just how frustrated I'd get

You made me wonder

Could there be more to what you are saying
Why do I feel that there's more to your story
You seem to be trying so hard, more than is normal
Time and time again, I wonder about you
You have this persona that makes keep thinking
Why you do, the things you do
Why you say, the things you say
It just doesn't add up, the way that it should
There's something that just doesn't fit
It feels like a puzzle, with a peace that's missing
What makes you, behave that way?
What makes you, look that way?
I look at you and I wonder, is it just me
But why do you seem to be trying so hard
Making me feel that I'm the one
Telling me in so many ways; to question myself
Why do you make me feel so unsure?
Or are you reflecting to me who you are
Is there something inside that you are hiding from me?
I think you know just what I mean
And now I know just what it is

What to do?

I look in to your eyes, and I see trouble
I see confusion and fear
Your mind is racing as you talk to me
You talk and talk your thoughts coming out
You keep looking to see my reaction
You want to see if I'm with you
Do I share your take on things?
But I just stare back at you
My eyes show no emotion
No, I dare not show any emotion
I've been there, I've done that
I know that what you need is help
Help that's is nothing that I can give
You need someone who knows
Someone with the knowledge I do not poses
So I just stare on, my body present
But my mind is not there
I cannot bear to listen, to you
Yet I am still there as you ramble on
From one topic to the next
I wish that you would stop
But you go on, making little sense of anything
I wish I could wave a magic wand
I wish I could make you well
But for now all I can do is stare
Stare at you as I blank my mind out
Blank it so I don't have to feel
To feel the pain that it does to me
Every time that I listen
Every time that I'm there

The Pain in My Heart

Nobody knows, the pain in my heart
Nobody knows, how much I cried
Nobody knows how, it tear's me apart
Nobody knows, my feelings inside
It's been so hard holding it all in my heart
When all I felt like doing is letting it out
When the tears in my eyes were burning inside
Just waiting to come, pouring down like the rain
Nobody knows, the pain in my heart
Nobody knows, how lonely I've been
Nobody knows, how it broke me apart
Nobody knows, my fear inside
Sometimes I ask myself so many whys
Why did it have to be me?
Why did I not see it coming?
Why did I be so naïve?
Why did I be so trusting?
But day after day, I have the same answerer
How could I have ever known?
When life had not prepared me yet
To never judge a book by its cover
Nobody knows, the pain in my heart
Nobody knows, how much I learned
Nobody knows, how I grew up so fast
Nobody knows, the new strength in my heart

I see your pain

When I look in to your eyes I see sadness
I see pain and confusion
You smile but your eyes do not smile
Your eyes have no glow
It's as though your soul knows no joy
The spirit without happiness
You're able to fool others
By the way that you smile
But I see the pain that you carry
I look in your eyes and I see your soul

Who are you?

Who are you?
Are you your shoes and your clothes?
Are you your house and your car?
Are you the money you spend?
Are you the gifts that you give?
Stop, take time and think
Who are you?
When you look in the mirror
Who looks back at you?
When you are a lone
When you sit in you room
Who sits there with you?
Are you happy with whom you see?
Do you see a person who cares?
A person with true love in your heart
If that's what you see and that's what you feel
Then you can be proud of whom that you are

Trouble with in

Your troubled mind has torn you inside
Like a splitting that's deep down within
It's been so hard holding most of your pain
For all the years it's been deep down within
And all the many breaking downs
I've tried so hard to find you away
Away to make it all go away
But nothing ever seems to help
It makes me so sad and I just need to cry
I cry for all the days
I cry for all the years
That keep coming and going by
With you in such pain
A mined of confusion
Was I to blame
Even though I know it's nobody's fault
But it's the feelings of despair
The sadness at heart
I wish they would help
Is there something I can do?
Or something I should say
Feelings of loss plague my heart
And I don't know what it is I should do
A heart full of pain please don't make me cry

My wish to you

If I had but one wish
I'd wish it off to you
If I had but one wish
I'd want that you were free
That all those things
That make you sad
And all those things that trouble you
Could leave your life forever
And set you free again
I'd make you have a brand new life
One filled with lots of peace
I'd make it have, such harmony
With no more noise
And no more pain
Just full of lovely melodies
And pleasant sounds to hear
Soon you would be back again
With a face so full of smiles
And the clouds you had
Would all gone away
Never to come again

When time stood still

Time and time again I look back
I drift on and on back, back, back
To a time so long ago
Yet it feels just like yesterday
A time when life stood still
A time when the world as I knew it changed
I was in shock
It felt like my heart was being ripped from my soul
It ached so badly like I had never known it could
My head was spinning as I tried so hard to make sense
To understand what was going on
How could this be, why me?
I was a good person, I cared about people
I loved my family, I prayed to God
And now my world was crashing down around me
I feel so weak, so weak that I have no voice
I open my mouth but no words come out
Tears pore down my face but no sound
I have no energy, no spirit, and no will

When you went away

I can remember that day so very clearly
The sun was shining, the birds were singing
It felts so good, life couldn't be better
Then came the news that would shock me to the core
You were to be no more
You had taken your very last breath
Suddenly life stood still
Was it a dream, would I wake up
I just wanted it to stop, please wake me up
But that never happened
I felt so confused, so scared, so sad
How could I ever go on?
Who would be there to hold my hand?
And show me all the wonders of the world
Who would make me laugh when I'm down?
I can feel the pain tearing me apart
It feels like I too am dying
I have no strength left in me
My head aches from all the crying
My voice is gone and my eyes are dry
No more tears left, I just stare
Looking, though I see nothing
Will I ever smile again?
Will the sound of birds bring me joy once more?
Will it make me feel so full of life and love?
Just the way it did before
Before you left me all alone
That day, the day you went to Heaven
To be with all the angels
I guess that's what you were
I guess that's what you are